LIVING THE DREAM IS...

By

Louise Hughes

Copyright © Louise Hughes 2017
This book is sold subject to the condition that it shall not, by way of trade or otherwise, be lent, resold, hired out, or otherwise circulated without the publisher's prior consent in any form of binding or cover other than that in which it is published and without a similar condition including this condition being imposed on the subsequent publisher.
The moral right of Louise Hughes has been asserted.
ISBN-13: 978-1979171007
ISBN-10: 1979171009

This book has not been created to be specific to any individual's or organizations' situation or needs. Every effort has been made to make this book as accurate as possible. This book should serve only as a general guide and not as the ultimate source of subject information. This book is intended only to educate and entertain. The author shall have no liability or responsibility to any person or entity regarding any loss or damage incurred, or alleged to have incurred, directly or indirectly, by the information contained in this book..

CONTENTS

INTRODUCTION *Living the dream is...* 1
1 ... *commitment and staying in the moment* 4
2 ... *taking a step back* 6
3 ... *living with source energy* 9
4 ... *doing what you love* 11
5 ... *knowing the glass is always half full* 13
6 ... *knowing love is all you need* 17
7 ... *practising yoga and breathing techniques* 19
8 ... *alternative therapies and natural health products* 24
9 ... *working with the law of attraction* 27
10 ... *using affirmations* 32
11 ... *having a wonderful day* 40
12 ... *loving, respecting and looking after number one* 43
13 ... *knowing your body is your temple* 46
14 ... *meditating* 49
15 ... *taking time to smell the flowers* 52
16 ... *practising the art of giving* 54
17 ... *knowing difficult people and challenges are our guides and blessings in disguise* 56
18 ... *practising forgiveness and letting go* 60
19 ... *sending a blessing* 66
20 ... *knowing love will always conquer fear* 71
21 ... *knowing love is eternal* 77
22 ... *knowing how to heal yourself* 82
23 ... *being true to yourself* 96
24 ... *knowing you are an evolving soul* 99
25 ... *detachment* 103
26 ... *knowing your life is a mirror image of your thoughts* 106
27 ... *knowing life is very simple (a shortcut)* 110
EPILOGUE 113

INTRODUCTION

Living the dream is…

What is living the dream? To most people it would mean living in a large, luxurious house, driving expensive cars, frequently taking exotic holidays and wanting for nothing.

Many people have all of this and much more, but are very rarely happy. That is not to say that money cannot make you happy; of course it can, to a point. But first you have to be happy from within – truly in your heart and soul – and then money is a bonus because it can give you more freedom to choose. Deep down we all know this, but some of us have become a little lost along the way in our search for happiness; we are just getting on with life, doing as we are told and making do with the cards we seem to have been dealt, but knowing in our hearts there has got to be more to it than this. Of course we have some great and happy moments, but life is meant to be fantastic all of the time, not just for a few moments. When we were young most of us lived this happy and carefree kind of life. As we get older we get on the treadmill and it just keeps turning. This book will show you how to get off the treadmill and fall in love with yourself and your life; how you can have a fantastic life and start to live the dream, not because you have material wealth, but because you have the wealth of knowledge.

If money is of interest to you then it will also show you how you can have as much money as you desire in your wildest dreams. The key is to have complete balance. You can never experience long-term outer joy from monetary or material wealth until you first find your inner joy.

The methods in this book may be quite new or controversial to some people, so please read with an open mind. If it works for you then go with it. If there are some chapters with which you do not agree then just let them go. We all have a choice so choose what appeals to you and simply let go of what doesn't. Remember, if you don't try the methods you will never know, so what have you got to lose? It won't cost you anything and there will be no side effects. You don't have to tell anyone… until you actually start to see the results for yourself!

This book is written for everyone. Whether you're young or old, rich or poor, from any background or beliefs. If you need a helping hand, feel lost and lonely, confused, afraid, or in pain. Whether you want to find the key to the door of your life or just know you are special and want to be able to shine.

It's all about changing your mindset and going with the

flow of your life and loving every moment you are given. At the beginning it does take commitment and effort until it becomes habit. If you just focus on one chapter you will see a change; if you focus on them all you will live in a magical world. When you live from your heart you feel great and love life and that is something that no amount of money can ever buy. That is when you are living the dream!

CHAPTER 1

Living the dream is… commitment and staying in the moment

To be successful at anything in life you have to be prepared to commit time and energy. It is impossible to succeed at something if you have not given time and effort. Any successful person will be happy to tell you their story of blood, sweat and tears to get where they are today! Many people commit and fight against all the odds to achieve success or to overcome an illness. To achieve anything in life you really have to commit. A half-hearted approach will give half- hearted results! There is no shortcut! If you are not happy in certain areas of your life, or maybe even all of your life, then that situation will not change until you change. You have to take responsibility and focus on the change you would like to see in your life, then commit and make it a habit. This book will give you all of the tools to achieve a wonderful life but it cannot do it for you. Only YOU can do it. Like any new tool it will take lots of practice and there will be challenges, but that is part of the fun. Remember, it takes around 30 days to form a habit. So in 30 days you could be a whole new you! As soon as you start to read this you will instantly see changes in your life. Most importantly, remember to stay in this moment. The only real time is now. What you do in the present moment has created your past and is creating your future. Be mindful of each and every thing that you do in each and every second and be sure to give everything to this moment because it is creating your life.

In brief:

To get the results you would like to see, you have to give time, commitment and energy.

Give everything to this moment because this very moment is creating your life.

CHAPTER 2

Living the dream is… taking a step back

In life we get wrapped up in situations, which is wonderful if it is a positive situation. It means we are absorbing all the energy in that moment and feeling great on an emotional and physical level. It is hugely beneficial to our health when we feel good because our endorphin levels increase which means we are releasing all of the right chemicals for a healthy and happy body. If we have an illness our body's healing process excels because the endorphin release helps our body to heal. On the opposite end of the spectrum, if our moment is a negative one, for example, if you are arguing, shouting, fighting, or in any situation that makes you feel bad, then the more you get wrapped up in that situation the worse it gets. You shout louder, the other person shouts louder and so it spirals. Or maybe you have a problem or situation you can't resolve and it's getting you down. Because you are so involved, the situation can seem impossible. It is at these times you need to take a step back or walk away and assess the issue from an outsider's point of view.

To some of us, escaping the situation may seem difficult. If you are in the middle of an argument, you are right and that person is wrong and you have to get your point across. The trick is this. As soon as you feel tension rising, instead of biting back or shouting, just walk away knowing negative and hurtful words are simply our ego. Say to yourself or, if you feel quite strong, look at them and say, "The truth lies within our souls." Calmly and gently smile then walk away, constantly repeating to yourself, "Peace, love and blessings," and keep smiling, you will immediately start to feel calmer. This may seem the complete opposite to what you want to do but it suddenly makes you feel amazing! Try it, there is no doubt it works. You feel calm because there is now no argument to have and the other person can't argue because you are in passive mode. It doesn't mean they or you have won the argument, but it defuses it so you can take time out to assess the situation. The reason you feel so good is because you have worked from your soul, not your ego, which immediately has a calming effect.

We all know how stressful it can be and how emotionally and physically drained we feel after arguing with spouses, etc. After coming out of the situation, sit down or find a quiet place and ask yourself for an answer. If you listen you will have the perfect answer. We are an evolving soul which means we will always have the perfect solution. The trick is to listen to your soul, not your ego. How do we know the difference?

Your ego will jump in with the answer – usually negative and it will be benefitting your ego and self. If it's your soul, you need to be still and at peace to receive the answer and it will come from your heart. It will feel right because it feels full of kindness and surrounded by love. Once you have the answer, work with it. Be patient and live from your heart.

In brief:

If you are in a positive situation, bathe in it and absorb all of the positive energy. It will make you feel good and is extremely beneficial if any healing process is needed.

If you are in a negative situation, immediately take a step back and assess it from your heart. It is not beneficial to be in that situation and will make you feel very low and negative.

CHAPTER 3

Living the dream is... living with source energy

What is source energy? Most of us have realised there is something greater than us. All religions are of the concept/belief there is a power that created us and governs us and it has been given many names.

Many people have detached themselves from religion due to all the controversy that surrounds it and started on their own quest to find whatever 'it' is. They may call themselves spiritual, which means they live with source energy at their own level and pace, simply knowing there is a pure energy of love. To work with that divine energy is to live from your heart and to be loving to everything and everyone in your life, including yourself. Absolutely anyone can become spiritual. There is only one ingredient and that is simply to live from your heart. Some people may still put a name to it – 'God' or 'Tao', 'The Divine', or 'All that is' – but most importantly it is to know we are evolving souls and have been given this life as a gift from source energy. Everything is energy, whether it is a living organism or a simple table. And all of this energy comes from one source. This source is love. To describe this energy is quite difficult because it is so powerful. On a small scale, it is that wonderful feeling when you cuddle your children or when you feel so overwhelmed with love it fills you up and brings tears to your eyes. When you start to live from your heart you are living with source energy. This is when you start to experience magical things in your life, simply because you are taking a step back and starting to look at things differently.

In brief:
Know that everything is source energy.
Work with source energy, which is to live from your heart.
Be sure to love everything in your life, most importantly yourself because you are the purity of divine source energy.

CHAPTER 4

Living the dream is... doing what you love

Do you do what you love? Yes? That's great. No? That's not so good. Most of us will book a holiday once, twice, maybe more per year and counting down the days is what helps us get through the daily slog. Some of us will take up a hobby and maybe once a week, off we toddle to golf, art class etc., looking forward to a couple of hours of fun. That's good, but life should be fun all of the time. Think of all the things you love to do and do them. What's stopping you? Do you dread going to work every day? Think of the career you would love to do and do it. Get the qualifications you need. Can you imagine loving going to work every day and getting paid for it? Don't start coming up with excuses – there is always a way. Remember, if you commit to something you will succeed. If you really want to do something, whether it's a new hobby, career or life, then simply focus and do it. The only thing that is stopping you is you.

Appreciation is also a quick way to kick-start happiness. How many times have you given thanks for your life? Most of us never appreciate anything like our car or electricity until it goes wrong, then suddenly we realise how amazing it is. Once it's fixed we quickly forget again. Now imagine going through the day giving thanks for everything and feel in your heart how grateful you are, this makes you feel amazing. Try it for an hour. Everything you touch, everything you do, every step you take, every breath you take, give thanks. By the end of that hour you will feel fantastic and blessed. Get your fix from your life now. Believe you are a millionaire in life because you are. Love your life by giving thanks. It really does put you on a high. Try it now! If you give thanks for everything in your life and also start to enjoy your hobbies and career, imagine how fantastic you will be feeling at the end of each and every day!

In brief:

Take up hobbies and pastimes that you really love and enjoy, and pursue a career that you've always dreamed of.

Be grateful for the life you already have and your gratitude will bring more good things into your life. You will start to see how really lucky you are.

CHAPTER 5

Living the dream is… knowing the glass is always half full

Are you a positive person? Most of us think we are. "Yes, I'm very optimistic," we all say. But are you really? Do you feel positive about absolutely everything in your life – your health, family and career? In our whole life, in every situation there are always two choices, two routes. It is completely black and white. Positive or negative. It's that simple. It is our choice which one we take. If you take the negative route then it doesn't take a genius to work out how you are going to feel about that situation. Everything related to it will be depressing, dark, and when you think about it or talk about it, on an emotional level it will make you feel low. On a physical level, depending on how bad it makes you feel, it is releasing all of the wrong chemicals into your body which will eventually manifest itself as an illness: headaches, ulcers etc. The alternative choice is the positive route. How do you think this makes you feel? No matter how bad the situation seems there is always a positive solution. Look for it, search for it. You will find it. Do not drown yourself in all the doom and gloom of the situation. Take a step up and search for every solution, have faith and believe. Research people who have succeeded in the situation you are in and it will give you the faith that is needed. Work with source energy, not against it, and remember to live from your heart.

Take a look at the people you hang out with. Are they full of fun and laughter or do they constantly drone on about all of their problems? Be aware of your home and environment. Are you surrounded by positive things in your home and workplace? Fill your home with all the things that make you feel happy and good inside: Flowers, plants, pictures, crystals. This has a huge effect on how you start your day. If you get up and are faced with depressing pictures or you dislike your curtains or bedding, it pretty much sets you up for a lousy day. Change it. Surround yourself and feel good about your home and start the day feeling great.

Get organised. There is nothing worse than living in chaos. If you have to spend half an hour manically searching for a shoe you pretty much play catch-up for the rest of the day. If you are really disorganised and feel overwhelmed by clutter then you really need to sort this out. Get however many boxes you need for each room and put all of the clutter in the boxes. Either put the boxes in a garage or shed, or if that is not available to you, stack them neatly in a corner of the room. Then gradually whenever you have the time – maybe set aside an hour a week – sort out one box at a time. Only keep what you need and feel good about either selling your items to someone who will appreciate them, or donate the rest to charity. You will feel so much better when you become organised.

Treat your home to a lick of paint. It practically costs nothing and it will completely transform a room. Love your home and it will love you back. You will transform the energy in your home and you will feel the difference immediately. We all know about people who talk to their plants, they are the most amazing gardeners. It is because they put love into their gardens. It is the same with anything in your life, whether it is your garden, your home, your partner, your children, your work. If you genuinely love it, it will love you back. However much energy you give out to something is the amount you will get back.

Lack of money is a very negative thing to a lot of people, but the very reason they lack it is because they have such negative feelings towards it. Worrying if they have enough to pay the bills or afford a holiday means all of their energy towards it is negative. People who have lots of money have a healthy respect for it and love what choices it gives them. You will not get more money until you change your mindset and respect and love what it can do for you. Many of us have been brought up seeing our parents worrying about paying for things so it is ingrained in our minds from childhood. All you have to do is change your attitude to money and start to enjoy and be grateful for the money you do have and suddenly more will start to come into your life. Love money in a healthy way and it will love you back.

In brief:

> *In every situation you have two choices, positive or negative.*

> *Be aware of your environment. Do your home and the people you hang out with provide a good and happy environment? If not, then you really need to work on this.*

> *Whatever energy you give out to something shows in the result you see. If you genuinely love your home, garden, work, health, family and finance it will love you back. What results do you see?*

CHAPTER 6

Living the dream is… knowing love is all you need

Love is all you need. That's it. It is that simple. If everyone lived from their heart and saw everything through the eyes of love, can you imagine how the world would be? We wouldn't need policing, government, insurances, keys to lock our doors and possessions, because everyone would be kind and caring. Isn't it amazing to think that we could all live in harmony if everyone lived from their heart? Remember, most of us do. Those who don't, it's not because they are evil but because they haven't been shown any other way. If you bring up a child in a pure loving home and he or she knows nothing other than pure love, then it is not possible for him or her to be anything else. If a child is brought up in hate and abuse then he or she knows nothing else and has no respect for themselves or anyone else. The one we have a problem understanding is the attention child who has been brought up in a so-called loving home, but the love has come from material possessions. Mum and Dad have fantastic careers, but have forgotten to give from their heart. Instead they give from their wallet. This child will do things to shock people as a cry for help and a way of getting attention, because they haven't fed their soul. Remember, love costs nothing. Be the change and know that everyone has a diamond within them. Some may be a little cloudy but all they need is to be shown the way to make them sparkle.

In brief:

Love is all you need for a perfect world. Be the change you want to see.

Realise everyone has a diamond within them. By showing others the way we can all start to shine.

CHAPTER 7

Living the dream is... practising yoga and breathing techniques

Yoga is amazing! Yoga will keep you in shape by improving blood circulation to the cells of the body, thus enhancing muscle tone. It massages your organs which improves digestion. It teaches you to breathe properly using the full capacity of your lungs. Awareness of breath in yoga reduces the breathing rate, heart rate and blood pressure, all of which will lead to improved wellbeing. Most importantly of all, it will help you find peace. Wow!

Anyone of any age can do it. Many of us have visions of our feet hanging down in front of our face like some amazing contortionist, but you can work within your own means, the most important part of yoga is the breathing. Try it a few times and you will not believe how grounded and peaceful it makes you feel. Always go to a reputable instructor, or purchase a DVD but make sure the DVD is by a qualified yoga instructor, not a fitness expert doing a bit of yoga. I have seen DVDs like this and they do not focus on the most important part of yoga: the breathing.

Breathing is very important. If we didn't breathe we wouldn't be alive! If you learn to breathe properly and practise deep breathing exercises the health and emotional benefits are huge. Breathing is our pump for the lymphatic system as the heart is our pump for the circulatory system. How deep we breathe determines how well our lymphatic system is working, which is how we get rid of all the toxins in our blood. It is our body's sewer system! If you are not exercising or deep breathing regularly then you will eventually get a build-up of toxins which will result in many health issues. Massage also plays a huge role in releasing the build-up of toxins. Read up the about the lymphatic system if you would like to find out more.

Deep breathing is the fastest way to trigger your parasympathetic nervous system, which is what practitioners call the relaxation response. So not only are you cleansing out your toxins but it also has a calming effect on your emotions.

Breathing techniques can also be used for spiritual cleansing. Some of you may have heard of chakras. It is an eastern belief that dates back thousands of years. Many therapies now work with cleansing and unblocking the chakras. There are thousands of chakras within us, but most therapies tend to work with the seven main chakras or energy centres. Emotions are believed to be held in the chakras and if they are not released then they can become imbalanced or blocked. They are seen as spinning vortexes of energy and each chakra has a relevant colour. Read up about chakras, some people believe they have a huge impact on our emotions and health.

A wonderful exercise to do daily is cleaning your chakras. Many people have amazing results from practising this technique. Firstly, you need to be aware of the relevant colour and location for each chakra.

Chakra	Name	Colour	Location
1st Chakra	Root Chakra	Fiery red	Between anus and genitals.
2nd Chakra	Sacral Chakra	Orange	Upper part of sacrum
3rd Chakra	Solar Plexus Chakra	Golden yellow	Two fingers above the navel
4th Chakra	Heart Chakra	Green/pink	Centre of chest (breastbone)
5th Chakra	Throat Chakra	Light blue	Between inner collarbone and larynx
6th Chakra	Third eye Chakra	Indigo	One finger above the nose centre of forehead
7th Chakra	Crown Chakra	Purple, violet	Centre of top of head

Chakra cleansing

1. Take in three deep breaths. Imagine each breath in through your nose is pure cleansing breath and each breath out through your mouth is any negative energy that may be held within you.
2. With each *in* breath starting at your Root Chakra, imagine cleaning your chakra with the breath. The *out* breath is releasing all the negativity held in that chakra. Take two or three breaths with each chakra. If there is an imbalance, for example you may have stomach problems etc., spend a little more time on the chakra close to that area.
3. When you have cleaned the chakra then imagine it as a spinning vortex and in its relevant colour, as the most beautiful colour you have ever seen.
4. Follow this process with each chakra, starting at the Root Chakra and working up in order to the Crown Chakra.
5. When you have finished on the chakras then imagine your whole body surrounded in a pure white/golden light.
6. Finish the exercise with three general cleansing breaths.

Just try this for one week and feel the difference!

Apparently we only use 20% of the capacity of our lungs. Find out about breathing techniques from valid sources and practise them daily. You will feel the benefits immediately.

In brief:

- *Practise yoga, the health benefits are astounding even if it's just 10 minutes a day.*
- *Yoga will help you find inner peace.*
- *Research and practise breathing techniques and help to clean your body's sewer.*
- *Practise cleansing your chakras daily.*

CHAPTER 8

Living the dream is... alternative therapies and natural health products

There are a vast selection of alternative therapies these days. Many of them are hugely beneficial to health and wellbeing and even GPs work closely with some as they are starting to see the amazing benefits. I have practised Reiki for many years and live in awe of the miraculous results on people and animals. Read up and research therapies in your area and take responsibility. Therapies will usually work from within and encourage the body to heal naturally rather than the more conventional way which may entail popping pills to mask the problem. The major plus to alternative therapies is the fact that there are no serious side effects. It always amazes me when people happily pick up their prescriptions with a leaflet as long as their arm telling them of all the possible serious side effects the drug can cause, to which most people respond by merely tossing the leaflet in the bin! I have nothing against modern medicine, but some really do have serious implications. At least try and work with natural alternatives as well, and if possible instead of. Try and change your diet to what is recommended for your condition. There is so much information now on the internet etc. Take responsibility. Research natural alternatives.

Only use reputable companies who can guarantee natural ingredients with quality and purity. Try different therapies and choose the ones that work best for you.

Why not book yourself on a nutrition course and become knowledgeable on the correct nutrients your body needs to live a long and healthy lifespan?

If you are receiving medication at the moment, do not stop. Work with your doctor and therapist and gradually try to introduce natural alternatives. All of us including practitioners are starting to become aware of this serious issue so your doctor should be more than happy to work with you in creating a healthier life.

In brief:

Research natural and alternative therapies and go with which ones suit you.

Become responsible for your health and don't expect a doctor to prescribe pills with serious side effects.

When you look for natural health products research companies who can guarantee you are getting the best quality.

Sometimes you may have to pay slightly more but it is your health that you are prioritising, not your wallet.

↣ Book yourself on a nutrition course.

CHAPTER 9

Living the dream is... working with the law of attraction

There are many books written on this subject. If you haven't heard of it before then you had better buckle up and hold on for the ride! This is a really exciting concept which suggests you are in control of your life through your thoughts. It means you have total control to shape your whole life in whichever way you want. So if you think your life is unfair, or you've been a victim of fate, then it is only so because of your thoughts. Of course we wouldn't consciously create a difficult life for ourselves but unconsciously, through prolonged thought patterns, we have created our perception of every situation in our lives.

The law of attraction works through our energy field. Everything is energy, including us. Under the most powerful microscopes in the world we are seen as matter, matter is composed of atoms. An atom is an energy form, therefore everything is energy. All energy has a frequency and will find the same frequency, which is where 'like attracts like' comes into the equation. Whatever our thoughts and beliefs are, they will be drawn to us through our own energy field, whether they are positive or negative. If we have one thought and that is all we focus on, then the universe will match that thought and it will materialise into our world. Everything in your world is brought to you and created through your thoughts and feelings, which is your energy. Take a look around you and look at what you have created through your thoughts.

This is 'the gift' of your life that source energy/God/the creator/the universe has given you. The magic to create your own world through your thoughts. Many people are aware of this concept, it has been around for thousands of years. Many people have never heard of it before. It is not kept for the special few or the chosen ones. Everyone has this gift. All you need is focus and belief and you can create anything in your world. For example, this is how top athletes achieve their goals. Their mind has complete focus on what they want to achieve. They are like a blinkered horse, nothing will deter them from their goal. It takes a huge amount of effort and belief but they know how the universe works. Their energy field has a frequency which is their thoughts and feelings and the universe will match that frequency to give them the result they asked for or believed in. If you completely believe, you will achieve. That is the law of attraction.

The important thing to remember is that we are here to enjoy life and to make the very best of this gift. We were never meant to suffer. At first this is a really scary concept, but when you realise what you're reading, this is suddenly the most exciting moment of your life. The wonderful thing about this is that it means we can create a life we had only ever dreamed of – the only key factor you need is belief and to be totally in line with the universe. To be in line with the universe means to be on the same level as the universe, which means to love your life and see and feel love in everything. You may say, "I know people who have achieved their goal but are certainly not in line with the universe and they certainly don't see love in everything." This is true but the difference is it will be short-lived and they will not experience inner joy from what they have created. They will always be searching and their achievements will be an empty victory.

To be in line with the universe takes practice. It means to daily give gratitude and love to everything in your life until it becomes habit. You cannot scream and shout and think and say negative things, then say a couple of positive words and thank-yous and think you are in line with the universe and an evolved soul. Make it become a habit. You cannot imagine how your whole world and everyone in it will change. You really need to practise this because the results are mind-blowing. It is like you are living in heaven on earth. Don't get stressed with yourself when you do lose it. Just draw a line under it and start again. As long as you are practising and trying, it will eventually become a habit.

You really need to focus and start to decide on the things you desire and the kind of life you would like to live. You deserve to live a wonderful and happy life. Don't feel guilty about wanting material things. It means you have ambition and it gives you something to strive for. The important thing to remember about money is that it is never your number one. You have to first love yourself and your gift of life. Only then can you appreciate money and the choices it can give you. As far as money is concerned, we all know it cannot buy you happiness, but if you are happy within then money may be an added bonus, to give you freedom to choose, maybe to travel etc. For many people money has no appeal and you would prefer a different life, like more time or peace. Read up as much as you can about this. There are many bestsellers written on the law of attraction and whether you believe in it or not, it is a law that governs your life so it is in your interest to work with it and create something amazing! You can change in an instant whatever it is you want, whether it's happiness, health, a partner, career, money. You can create the life of your dreams. This is one of the most amazing things you will ever read because all of the power is literally in your hands.

If you find this notion hard to grasp then do a bit of research on people who have succeeded against all the odds. Each and every one of their stories will tell you they got there by believing and focusing on what it was they wanted to achieve. Every ounce of energy and thought will have taken them to their destination. Nobody achieves their ambitions or fulfils their dreams by chance. They get there through commitment and belief in themselves and their dream.

When you begin to realise this, you can then start to decide what kind of life you really want to live. Many people have a dream book which is where you cut out pictures of things that you have always dreamed of, for example your dream holiday, car, home, garden or anything which appeals to you. It may just be a picture of someone sitting in the middle of a field on a beautiful day which to you represents peace and time. Place them in a form of scrap book and if you like you can put dates next to the pictures for when you want them to materialise and become your reality. Or some people have a dream board (cork board) for all the pictures and put it in a place where they can see it every day. You then look at them as often as possible and get really excited about receiving all these wonderful things and this wonderful new life.

The next chapter will show you how to use the law of attraction with affirmations.

In brief:

The law of attraction is one of the laws of the universe whether you believe in it or not. It is governing your life through each and every thought that you make.

Research the law of attraction and people who have worked with this concept.

Decide on the things or life you would love and make up a dream book or board.

CHAPTER 10

Living the dream is... using affirmations

An affirmation is a short, powerful statement that you say to yourself. It is a positive statement, to counteract a negative belief. Have you ever tried this? Think of something you feel negative about, for example: "I feel fat and ugly," is quite common amongst us ladies. Then say to yourself the opposite positive words: "I feel slim and beautiful." Now I'm guessing that almost all of you are either laughing or saying, "Yeah, right," but this really does work. As with everything, try it and see for yourself. The key here is you have to believe, otherwise it doesn't work. Really understand what I'm saying here. You have to believe. What you need to realise is 'to believe' and 'to want' have two completely different meanings. If you 'believe' something then that means in your world that is the absolute truth with no doubts whatsoever. To 'want' something means you desire or crave something to be yours, therefore, you are not actually believing it to be so. You are wanting and wishing it to be so, which means it will always be in the future tense.

First you have to write or think of your affirmation. I recommend writing because it gives it a physical existence. Remember, you have to be very specific on what it is you want. If your desires are wishy-washy and not specific then the results will be wishy-washy. Then imagine what it would be like, for example, to be slim and beautiful or have a perfect career or partner. You have to believe in that moment you are actually there and genuinely feel it in your heart. You have to 'act as if'. Once you've imagined it and really felt what it feels like, use that feeling when you say the affirmation. The more you believe it the quicker the results come. Believe you deserve it. This is where many people fail in achieving their goals. Doubt is a major contributor in your dream not materialising. It is sometimes a good idea to keep your wishes to yourself because other people's negativity can inspire doubt. You have to feel genuine love for whatever you desire, not greed or lust, because that is something completely different and is not in sync with the universe.

If you have pictures in your book or on your board then look at them and really feel yourself in that place right now. If you want to lose weight then have a picture of you when you were slim, or cut out a picture of your head and put it on the picture of the body you want. Look at it every day and before you go to sleep and truly believe it is you. You will actually start to become that person. If you find this too difficult to accept, just try it. You have nothing to lose, you don't have to tell anyone, but it is so exciting when people start to comment on how different and great you look. You will automatically start to eat more healthily and become aware of fitness because fitness and health come hand in hand with your perfect body. If you commit and believe then you may start to see results in around 30 days! It is so exciting!

Even if you are going through a difficult time in your relationship or job, if you start to imagine how good it could be and you focus and believe it, then it becomes your reality. It is amazing to use with your partner. Many of us start to become complacent in our relationships and yearn for that spark we once had. Or we feel our partner has become selfish and lazy and we tend to only see them as being negative. If you want to watch them transform into your perfect partner, then all you have to do, for 30 days only, is to focus on the good things about them (if you feel they haven't got any, then remember why you got together and what it was that appealed to you). Write these down and keep saying to yourself how amazing and how wonderful they truly are. Only focus on the positives, do not acknowledge the negatives, but as with all these concepts it has to genuinely be from your heart. If you stick to this they will literally change before your very eyes like magic!

As you can see this is a very simple process. You simply:

1. *Decide what you would like, write it down, being very specific and putting it in the present tense. Thank you for my wonderful… e.g. health.*

2. *Ask the universe for your wish.*

You do this by saying your affirmation and imagining it being your reality now, as you are saying it. As you ask, you must believe you are there in the moment with whatever it is you want, and you have to feel the excitement. The universe works on energy, so your feelings play a major role. You have to feel the excitement you would feel if it was here now. If you think of your wish but have no feeling connected to it then it cannot materialise.

Do not wonder *HOW* you will get it. Because when you question *HOW* it will appear, the wish or thought is immediately sent back because you lost faith. We are brought up to think logically so we feel we have to know *HOW* it will appear. You have to let it go and trust the universe. Always start with something small so that your brain can adjust to this method. Over a period of manifesting lots of little things, you will start to acknowledge it is far more than coincidence and realise you are actually creating through your thoughts. Once you have convinced the logic in your brain you are the creator, you can go on to create bigger things.

3. *Let it go* and KNOW it is coming to you. The KNOWING is the actual granting of the wish. If you do not KNOW it is coming then it cannot appear in your world. It is like believing but it is one step further. The difference in believing and knowing is, a belief is something you believe in, but it is open to change. A knowing is something far deeper. A knowing comes from deep within your soul. To know something involves your mind, body and soul and it is a

connection to source energy.

This is probably the most difficult part, you can imagine what you want but then stress about how it can materialise and then add doubt which immediately sends your wish back.

You have to imagine it first, then absolutely KNOW it will appear. You have to carry on with your life having complete confidence the universe will grant your wish.

Many, many people fail on this step and lose faith and say, "What a load of nonsense!" When you have done steps 1-3 you have to let go. By holding on to it as a wish, that is all it will ever be. You have to let it go to materialise. Let it go with the absolute belief and faith it will now appear into your world. It may appear through an unexpected source, so be open to any possibility. For example, you may think you would like £5,000 so go and buy a lottery ticket because that's the only way you think you can get it. But you must let go because you are not in control of it, the universe is. As long as you have an unwavering faith and a KNOWING, then it will arrive. It may just appear or you may be nudged in a certain direction. It will feel right from within if it's the universe guiding you. Be aware of situations that may be presented to you by the universe in your life and go with them.

4. *Receive and give thanks.*

Always give thanks. Give thanks when you ask for your wish and when you receive your wish. You can never thank the universe enough for what it has given you. Your gratitude should be given daily with every breath that you take. The universe has given you life. Gratitude in life determines what kind of life you lead. The more genuine gratitude you have for your life, the more you will be given to be grateful for.

You can create absolutely anything. Remember, this is not a new concept to you. You have been doing this process every day of your life, you just haven't been conscious of it. You had a thought, presumed and knew it would happen and it did. What you now realise is by changing the thought you can change the outcome. Whatever your situation is now, it is merely the result of your past thoughts and actions. By changing your thoughts right now your life can change. If you can visualise it then it can materialise. This is because whatever you can visualise already exists in the universe, you just can't see it, all it requires is your energy. Whether it's your dream car or a healthy version of you. All you have to do to bring it into your world is have complete focus and to act as if you already have it with your feelings of joy. That is the energy it requires to become your reality.

Try and set aside at least ten minutes, three times a day, for really focussing on your ambitions. You can also think about them as you go about your day and before you know it, it will be your reality! Remember, when you think of them it has to be in the present tense, in the now, in this very moment you are driving your dream car or being the person you want to be. And don't give up. It does work, but as with everything you need to commit. Give it at least 30 days and you should get a result or start to see change. How quickly the results come depends upon your belief, so remember, the more belief you have, the quicker the result.

If you think this doesn't work, then because that is your belief, you will be right. It won't work because whatever you truly believe is always right in your world. You have to have faith. Don't let people convince you it's a load of nonsense, let them live their lives. If you work with the concepts in this book you can create the life of your dreams. Why would you let the doubters talk you out of it? All you need is absolute faith and belief in yourself.

The one important thing to remember about the law of attraction is if you use it in a negative way, the negativity will come straight back to you. If you start to think negative thoughts and beliefs about other people, a negative situation will arise.

If you are a sports person and winning is your aim, do not focus on the other team or person, hoping they lose, because losing will appear in your life. Just focus on following your passion. If it's running then as long as you're following your heart and it's your passion you will be successful. Just see yourself winning and following your dreams. Do not focus on the opposition. This is how perfect the universe is. The universe is like a mirror – every thought is reflected back into your life, whether you're thinking that thought about yourself or someone else. The more energy you put into that thought, the quicker it comes into your life, whether it's a positive or negative energy. If you start to worry about this then know it has been proven scientifically that a negative thought is far less powerful than a positive thought, so if you catch yourself thinking negative thoughts don't start to panic. It can only materialise over a prolonged period and with a huge amount of energy. Just start to train your brain in a positive mindset and keep telling yourself, "I only have positive thoughts." Think of positive things about yourself and other people. Genuinely wish people the best in life and of course it will be returned to you by the universe, but always remember, it has to be genuine or it means nothing. You will be blown away by how many positive things start to show up in your life. You will be blessed tenfold.

Remember, when you live from your heart the universe will grant your every wish. But when you deter and start to think and talk negatively, you are not in sync with the positive vibes of the universe. You are now on a negative energy level which means only negative things will materialise.

Stay positive, and when you see your dreams turned into reality always give thanks and be truly grateful to the universe.

In brief:

Write down your affirmations and be specific.

Really imagine what it would be like to be the person you want to be, or drive your dream car and feel the excitement.

Know that when you are living from your heart the universe will grant your every wish.

CHAPTER 11

Living the dream is... having a wonderful day

Do you smile to yourself all day long? If not, why not? Well, most of us only smile if something makes us smile. It is a reactive response which means we feel happy. If we see someone walking alone smiling we tend to think they're a bit odd!

Put a big smile on your face right now. How do you feel? It feels good, yes? That's because when you smile you have an emotional change in your body, but it has to be a genuine smile. A fake smile has no effect. Try both and feel the difference. Now here is your challenge for the day: Smile all day long! If this seems impossible (because to some of us it would seem ridiculous to be happy and smile all day long), then firstly try it for a whole hour. Do you think you could manage that? So for one whole hour (or if you're feeling brave one whole day) then just smile. Just think about all the great things in your life and give thanks and a smile for them. And if you think, *Well, I haven't got that much to smile about*, then just smile and be grateful for your family, your friends, your home, your sight, your health or each and every breath that you take. The effect of smiling for this long, even if you just do it for the hour, is quite staggering. You will feel fantastic and it has a knock-on effect on the people you come into contact with. If you are not normally a smiley person it is so funny to see your partner or family's faces when they see you walk around the home smiling all day. It is so much fun just driving along and other drivers look at you and smile back. Or walking down the street, everybody smiles back or some look at you as though you're a bit odd and that not only makes you smile, it makes you laugh. Even if you don't come into contact with people, just smile while you're doing your chores or working on your computer. The wonderful thing here is that because your mindset is happy, then all the things that happen in the time you are smiling are actually all happy things.

This also has a huge effect on the healing process. If you are in pain or have an illness the last thing you want to do is smile, but try it. It is unbelievable how much better you feel. (There is also a scientific explanation for this. When you smile or are happy, endorphins are released which contain a chemical which is a natural painkiller.) You don't have to have a great big cheesy grin (although please feel free if that appeals to you), just a genuine contented smile will suffice. You are now creating a great day for yourself. The mind-blowing part of this is the huge effect it has not only on your day – for example maybe you get discounts, or all the traffic lights turn to green, or you get a perfect parking place – but on the people you come into contact with. Suddenly everyone is very amenable and I cannot emphasise enough how simply smiling has such a profound effect on your general wellbeing and health. Try it. It really is fantastic. You really do start to get a fix off this, which is why people think you're on something. And you actually are. It's called: The 'smiley high'.

In brief:
Smile as often as you can.
Smiling creates a chemical change in your body which immediately makes you feel better.
Your smile has to be genuine or it has no effect.
Watch the amazing effect your smiling has on your day and all the people around you, and most importantly of all your health and wellbeing.

CHAPTER 12

Living the dream is… loving, respecting and looking after number one

Now most of you will think, *Well how selfish is that?* But you couldn't be further from the truth. There is a saying – "By looking after number one you can then happily look after number two, three, etc." People who are happy within themselves know the key is to look after yourself and do the things you love to do. Set aside at least one day a fortnight and do whatever you love to do for as much of the day as possible, even if you can just manage an hour. Maybe a massage, sauna, or just a simple leisurely walk. The more relaxing the better. It feels wonderful to know you have a treat day to look forward to especially for you. I know this can be really difficult if you have small children or relatives to look after. If it is difficult to take time out, then you are the very person who must make an effort to do this because you need it more than anyone.

Treat yourself and love your life, then when someone asks you for help, or your family make their demands, you are more than happy to help. You feel great and your health is good because you are looking after yourself. If you do not look after yourself and put yourself at the bottom of the list, prioritising every man and his dog, how do you think you feel when people ask you for help? You feel low because you have nothing to look forward to and you will become resentful because you are doing nothing but giving. If you are not replenishing yourself you will have nothing left to give. Then you wonder why you feel exhausted and depressed and usually end up taking a trip to the doctor which results in a prescription for anti-depressants.

Many people feel they are victims in life and they are, purely because they have no respect for themselves. If you do not love and respect yourself you can guarantee nobody else will. You have to love and respect yourself and the immediate knock-on effect is that everyone else will too. Watch how popular people hold themselves. Their mannerisms have a confidence. Learn to love yourself. It is not in any way selfish. Appreciate all your qualities. If you feel bad things have happened in the past through either your fault or someone else's it is, as it says, in the past, it has gone. Move on and make changes. Act right now and immediately become the person you want to be. If you have been through a major trauma and it is holding you back then it is extremely important to let go because this will manifest within you and dictate your life. Read chapter 18 on forgiveness and letting go. From this very second, realise what a special person you are. Go to your mirror, look yourself in the eyes and say, "I love you," from the bottom of your heart. You may laugh the first time, or many of you may cry. It is very simple, love yourself and your gift of life.

In brief:

- *Set aside some 'me' time.*
- *People will only love and respect you when you love and respect yourself.*
- *If you feel the past is holding you back then it is important to let it go.*

CHAPTER 13

Living the dream is… knowing your body is your temple

We have all heard this saying many times but what does it actually mean?

Well, as it says, your body is a place of worship. Not in a vain way but in a respectful way. Your body is your loyal servant. It does everything it can to keep you healthy. It really is quite miraculous how it works but the only time many of us actually appreciate it is when we are sick and we want to feel healthy again. Usually we only appreciate it for a little while after we regain our health, then we soon forget. Usually while we are sick we blame our body and wonder why it is doing this to us. Sometimes we may even loathe it for what we feel it is doing to us. We need to realise our body is a miraculous thing. It is a wonderful gift we have been given. It is our transport in this life and much more. Through our body we can express our feelings and emotions. We have our five senses to touch, feel, taste, smell and to see this wondrous world. Our body is our loyal servant which stays with us to the end of this life and all it does is devote itself to our needs. From healing small cuts and scratches, to major forms of healing recovering from cancers, accidents and diseases. Without our body we cannot exist in this world. So to say, 'look after it' seems pretty much common sense, doesn't it? But how many of us actually are conscious and aware of our body daily? Do you only eat a healthy and nutritious diet? Do you take regular exercise? Do you only put natural products on your skin? Most of us seem more aware of how we are damaging our body rather than focusing on looking after it.

To smoke or put toxins and poisons in your body, it goes without saying that you are drastically shortening your lifespan. Treat your body with respect. It is only you who can do this, take responsibility. Can you imagine how much you would save the NHS or your health insurance if you actually looked after your body properly? Why wait and put your body through the major trauma of an operation or take pills for the rest of your life, after which the side effects will probably kill you before the actual health issue does?

Now some of you may say, "Well, my friend was really fit and healthy and she had a terrible disease." In response to that there is one major thing a lot of us don't realise. To look after your body is to do so not only on a physical level but also on an emotional level. Any doctor will tell you stress can cause many physical conditions. Prolonged stress can cause major physical conditions. Stress is an emotion that you feel. Change that emotion. That's all you have to do. Always look for the positive. Whatever the trauma you are going through there is always a solution. Take that route. If you want to stay healthy you only have that choice. If it involves something that has happened in the past you have to let go. Read chapter 18 on forgiveness and letting go. If it involves someone you care about who is suffering, a close member of the family or friend who themselves are going through a difficult time, then read chapter 19 on sending a blessing. You cannot be of any help to yourself or anyone else if you do not look after yourself. How can you help someone if you constantly talk morbidly about a situation? Take responsibility, search for the positive and work with it. Live your life in your wonderful body, it is a gift you have been given. Appreciate and respect it.

In brief:

- *Your body is your temple – treat it with respect.*
- *Become aware of your diet and how you treat your body.*
- *Remember, stress can also cause physical conditions so practise stress release daily, e.g. meditation.*
- *Invest in an atlas of the human body and read up how truly miraculous the human body is.*

CHAPTER 14

Living the dream is... meditating

Before you all start to roll your eyes, read this chapter all the way through because meditating is a shortcut route to finding complete inner peace, and it only takes a few minutes a day.

Anyone can meditate, you don't have to be a spiritual guru to feel the benefits. To meditate daily is hugely beneficial because it means your mind has a holiday every day! How great is that? All you need to meditate is peace and quiet for a few minutes a day. If you really think there is never a few minutes' peace at home then find a special place in your garden, a field, even sit in your car. But somewhere you won't be disturbed.

There are many forms of meditation: lighting a candle, listening to a meditation CD, finding a local group – choose which one works best for you. But the simplest way to get started is to find a quiet place, sit in a relaxed upright position, and simply breathe at a slow, relaxed pace and all you do is focus on the breath. Breathe in, breathe out. Breathe in, breathe out. Breathe in, breathe out. Thoughts may wander in at the beginning, you can acknowledge them if you want, but don't spend too long on them as the whole point of the exercise is to completely empty your mind, so when you are ready just gently push them away. As you progress you will become more and more relaxed – this is when you start to enter the meditative state. You may see colours which may be quite vivid but don't worry if you don't, just enjoy the relaxing experience. It is like anything, it will take practise and commitment. When you start to reach a totally relaxed state this is a perfect time to say your affirmations because your brain is in theta mode and the subconscious becomes aware of suggestions. Remember to always keep them positive and always say them in the present tense. For example, if you want to feel more confident you would say, 'I am feeling extremely confident.'

A few minutes' meditation a day is plenty, ideally about 10-20mins. You do not need to go into hours or you may feel spaced out for the rest of the day. Just enjoy it as a little mini holiday for your mind. You will be amazed at how much easier you can cope with the day ahead.

Once you commit and start to meditate regularly you will find you cannot live without meditation. It becomes your escapism in this manic world. It plays such an important role in your spiritual self because when you meditate, it connects you completely to source energy which is why you feel such an overwhelming sense of love and peace. It is the greatest high that you will ever get. In life, we search for happiness and things that make us feel good. All of these feelings are on a physical level and we may feel good for a while but it will never satisfy our soul. So when we find peace within, that is pure satisfaction. We feel at one with source energy, we feel completeness, our souls know it is where we have come from and it is where we will go back. When we meditate we are feeding and nourishing our soul, that is why we feel such peace and tranquillity within when we meditate. It is like a mini trip home to pure love.

Meditation is an absolute necessity in today's world. It is the way to find complete peace within yourself.

In brief:

Meditation plays a major part of finding inner peace.

Daily practice is strongly recommended. Just a few minutes a day is far more beneficial than an hour once a week.

Join a local group or research different ways of meditating and go with whichever one suits you.

CHAPTER 15

Living the dream is… taking time to smell the flowers

Look at all the beautiful things in this world and enjoy them. When you look around, you will start to see how truly blessed you are. How many times do you walk past your roses and actually take the time to inhale their spectacular perfume? Look at the magnificence of the trees, the history they have witnessed, how people must have lived when the oak tree was but a mere sapling. Appreciate everything and begin to feel overwhelmed at the beauty around you. Nothing is more perfect than Mother Nature herself. Invest in a bird feeder and watch the different varieties of little birds that come into your garden every day. Look at their tiny perfect bodies, their little matchstick legs. How miraculous that they can make a perfect home to raise their young ones purely by threading small sticks and bits of wool with their beaks.

Look at the world through the eyes of a child in absolute

wonder. Not just the perfection of nature but also inventions made by man. The genius of Henry Ford and the motor car. Einstein and science, Alexander Bell and the telephone. Look at the architecture of buildings. Be inspired. Be amazed at the glory around you. You are truly blessed to have been given this life, appreciate it in every second that you have. When you stand in a queue don't stand there puffing and panting with impatience. Look around you at the building and its contents and think how each item would have started as one person's imagination which was then made reality. Look at all the people and appreciate and respect that they all have such individual and unique lives. Genuinely give thanks daily for your life and you will not believe how much more you are given. You suddenly start to look at things differently and realise that there is magic all around you.

In brief:

Take the time to smell the flowers.

Appreciate and respect all of the wonderful things that surround you.

Give thanks daily for the perfection of nature and all of the wonderful things created by man.

CHAPTER 16

Living the dream is… practising the art of giving

To give from the heart is unconditional love in the purest form. It is a connection to source energy which is why the giver benefits even more than the receiver. They feel the purity of genuine love.

Do you only give presents on birthdays and celebrations? Or because you feel obliged? Give from your heart and feel the difference. It has been proven scientifically that the giver has a higher endorphin response than the receiver! Which means you gain a huge supply of happy chemicals by giving from your heart. It doesn't have to be an expensive material gift. It could be flowers from your garden, goodwill vouchers (e.g. babysitting, helping in the garden, housework etc.), but do it spontaneously. Any time you meet up with a friend or relative, your local shopkeeper or hairdresser. Give to charities, not just money but a bit of time. But remember it has to be genuine, from your heart, or you will not feel the rewards. If you practise this gesture regularly you will be amazed by how fantastic you feel, and the most amazing part is the more you give, the more you receive. This is how perfect the universe is. But the point to remember is that if you give to receive it doesn't work, if you genuinely give from your heart unconditionally then the universe will always bless you.

In brief:
➢ *To give from the heart is unconditional love in the purest form.*
➢ *The giver gets an even higher endorphin release than the receiver.*
➢ *Let giving become part of your life.*

CHAPTER 17

Living the dream is... knowing difficult people and challenges are our guides and blessings in disguise

No, really, they are! We all have a purpose in life – to live from our hearts. When we live from our heart we love life and life loves us. When difficult people and challenges come along, all they are doing is helping us to progress in life. They want us to live from our heart, they test us and challenge us. We know we have evolved when they are no longer an issue to us, because we are living from our hearts, not our ego. Behind every difficult challenge in life is a golden door waiting to be opened but we have to get through the challenge first before the door can be opened. Of course it can be difficult and that's why we are here; it's all about the journey, not the destination. So as the saying goes, 'enjoy the ride'. A question you should always ask yourself is, "Does it really matter?" In all the grand scheme of things, "Does it really matter?"

Next time someone winds you up, thank them because they are helping you progress. I have a wonderful husband and four fantastic children to thank because they help me to grow daily. Originally of course I had a slightly different view to say the least, but now I know I will be forever indebted to them. If someone is really winding you up use the method and words in chapter 2. All families and life are a wonderful challenge. Don't get wrapped up in your ego, use the tools in this book and have fun. Don't beat yourself up if you do falter along the way, there is always this very moment to change. We have to make the best of a situation. In comparison to a nun, monk or spiritual guru who can simply meditate or pray in a sanctuary, we have to deal with screaming, fighting kids or a demanding husband or wife, which is a tough environment and a major challenge. But that is our test, and how wonderful we truly are for being able to cope in this demanding environment, even though it doesn't always feel like it.

A good tip in a difficult situation is to 'rise above it'. It means to come out of the situation. To take a step back and imagine you are just your soul with no body and no ego. When that person or situation is testing you, look at the scenario as if you were just a soul. How would you deal with it then? Suddenly you look at the situation from a totally different perspective. You realise they are on their journey but they can no longer affect your journey, because you now have no ego. Or you may find them quite humorous because you can also see them as a soul and know that they are really your loving guide who is merely testing you and helping you to grow.

If you really are suffering, for example an extremely challenging partner where emotional or physical abuse is involved, then you always have a choice, you are always in control. You owe it to yourself to be happy, and if happiness isn't with them then find another place.

Another thing to remember is that you mustn't get hung up on other people's justice. In life on the surface, some things do appear to be unfair. Where certain people seem to 'get away with things'. Where they may live a so-called fantastic lifestyle, but you know they have got there illegally. Or they may not be very kind and have taken advantage of people, yet seem to be extremely lucky or affluent.

Know now, this very moment, that the universe has everything in hand. As I have mentioned in chapter 10, using affirmations, the universe is exactly like a mirror. Whatever you give out in life, it is reflected back into your own life. It may not be the exact thing but it will be on the same energy level. So if you give out negativity it will come back into your life. If you give out positive energy it will come back into your life. You may look at these people and think life's unfair but you do not know how they truly feel inside, or what traumas are going on behind their closed doors. Not that you should seek solace in this, because if you want negative things to happen to people it will be reflected in your life. But just know the universe is perfect and has it in check. Some people call this Karma, or 'what goes around comes around'. This doesn't mean that all people who have negative things happen in their life are bad people. But if their energy level is negative, whether it is through their thoughts and actions or in wrongdoing, then negative things will keep showing up in their lives. So just let it go and have faith in source energy and focus on living your life.

It can really take a while for some people to grasp this. Some people are forever moaning about family issues or how unfair their lives are and other people seem so lucky. Of course the negativity will just keep coming back into their life. Once you are able to let it go and know that divine source energy has it all in hand then you can start to focus positive energy in your life. Simply focus on enjoying your own life.

In brief:

Know that every difficult person and situation are wonderful blessings. Without them we would never be able to grow.

Try and come out of the situation and see it through the eyes of your soul, then they or it can no longer affect you because you are no longer responding with your ego.

Don't get het up about other people's justice. The universe has it in check. If they are giving out negativity in words or actions it will be reflected back into their lives. This is the sure-fire law of the universe, which is why the law of attraction is so perfect. By you getting worked up about them it will be reflected back in to your life. Let it go.

CHAPTER 18

Living the dream is… practising forgiveness and letting go

I have referred to this chapter on many occasions because it is probably the most important chapter to read in the book.

We all have challenges in life. It is to help us to evolve as souls. We bumble through them, coping in the best way we can. Some of us have friends and family who help ease the burden, some of us don't. But we all seem to eventually come through them. Some of us respect them and feel we have grown through the experience but some of us just can't let go. A childhood trauma is usually carried through into our adult life and sits within us. We try not to talk about it but now and again it rears its ugly head and brings back all of those traumatic, painful memories. Some of us lock it up completely and never dare go there. A childhood trauma is different to an adult trauma because a child does not have the tools to take responsibility to deal with a difficult situation and will look to their parent or guardian for a solution. That is the role of an adult but if it is the adult who is causing the trauma, or is in no fit state to help the child, then the child has nowhere to go, carrying confusion or blaming themselves. This really is a deep-rooted trauma because it has never been released and is carried for many years, even lifetimes. I have seen people in their late eighties still break down because of incidents that happened during their childhood.

If a trauma has happened in our adult life and we can't let it go, we tend to have feelings of anger or bitterness towards that person or situation.

None of this is in any way good for us. Firstly, it causes us pain and anguish when we think of it and secondly, it can literately eat away at us. As described in chapter 13 – your body is your temple. Stress causes physical imbalances and over prolonged periods it will cause major physical issues. So the key here is as it says, to forgive and let go. Not to release them but to free you. It is you who is suffering. It is you who drags the chains daily.

This process works no matter how traumatic the issue, use it and set yourself free, don't let the pain own you anymore. You deserve to live the life of your dreams and nothing and no one can ever hold you back. You have been given this life as a gift. It is not meant to be painful and a struggle. Don't feel guilty about feeling bitter, it is very easy for anyone to say, "Let it go," but there obviously has been a major upset for you to carry this pain, and you feel you have been very wronged. The important thing to understand is it is 'you' that is suffering and only 'you' can relieve that suffering. It is completely in your hands to free yourself.

To begin the process you will need a pen and paper. First of all start to write down your anguish, write how it makes you feel, write as many swear words and strong feelings and emotions as you can. If it is a person who has upset you then you can also write a separate letter to them to tell them how it made you feel, how much you hated them and what they did to you. Tell them everything and again, swear as much as you like if it helps you express the anger more.

Now what you have done here is released these feelings onto the paper, you have given it a physical existence. You may, if you like, read it aloud or imagine you are reading it to them. You can do this process as often as you feel the need. It may only take the one time or you may need to do it many times.

Now the next part of the process is of utmost importance. It is imperative that you follow this step.

You must destroy the paper and all of the written words. Because all of these painful memories are released from you and held on the piece of paper, they have been given a physical form. The best way is to burn it, but only where it is safe to do so. If this is not possible then shred it, but none of the words must exist. As you destroy it, see and imagine all of that pain going with it being taken away and being blessed in the purity of the universe, never to return.

Then give thanks to the universe for showing you the way.

Remember, these people who have caused you pain will have had a traumatic incident or horrific childhood themselves. They carry so much pain that they have not released it. They will have no respect for themselves so they certainly will have no respect for other people. This does not excuse them for what they have done and the pain they have caused, but it may help us to understand why they may do these things. They have a long journey ahead of them and have a lot to learn. Like us, they all have souls but sadly as of yet cannot hear them, they listen only to the anger inside their pain. Eventually they will remember, but that is their journey, not yours. Do not worry about their justice, only focus on setting yourself free.

Once you have done this process any physical ailments connected to this issue will also shortly disappear.

It is always a good idea after you have done this process to send a blessing – chapter 19.

How to forgive when you really hate someone:

You know when you really hate someone because you are thinking of them most of your waking hours. You cannot believe how they have treated you and the very thought of them and what they have done literally is making your blood boil and your heart pound. Your anger is raging inside of you and you feel like you could quite easily plunge a knife through their heart (although hopefully you do still have a conscience to stop you fulfilling this desire).

The reason there is so much hate is usually because there was once love, and that is why it hurts so badly. You have to release this hate because if it goes on for a long period it will surely take your health, sanity or both. If the hating has gone on for over a month it has now become a habit. You now have to consciously start to think happy thoughts continually, until that then becomes your habit. To some of us the hating feels good. You have to get out of this cycle. This can be hard work but you have to do it to break the negative thoughts.

The way to end this hate is to 'cut the cord'. Everything and everyone is connected to us in life and a simple way to visualise this is to imagine it as a cord. If someone is upsetting you so much that you feel only hatred towards them, then this will eat away at your very soul. You have to release them from you.

1. Imagine a picture of them connected to you by a cord.
2. Now take scissors and cut the cord, either in your mind or you can take a piece of string and cut it if you want to hear the sound of the scissors cutting the cord.
3. As you cut the cord say, "In love and light I cut the cord of negativity that connects us."
4. Now say, "Thank you. I am free and am no longer connected to you."

After you have cut the cord you will immediately feel a lifting sensation because you have cut the negativity from your life. You have raised your vibrational level and will now find it

LIVING THE DREAM IS...

far easier to work with the universe and fulfil your dreams.

You have an amazing life to live, live it!

You are now completely free of them. They may come back into your life after this process but only if *you* wish and only through a positive connection. Always send blessings and always say positive words.

Work with the methods in this chapter which are relevant to you at this moment in time. You can use them as often as you feel the need.

In brief:

Any emotional trauma will cause pain and eventually will manifest physically.

Use the methods in this chapter as often as you like until you feel you are free of the issue. It may only need to be done once. In the first method always remember to destroy the paper each time.

Remember, people who cause pain have usually suffered in their childhood. This does not excuse them for what they have done but it may help us to understand why they may do these things. Not to release them but to release ourselves.

CHAPTER 19

Living the dream is... sending a blessing

This is a very powerful chapter to read, so try and read a few times until you fully understand how it works.

In the dictionary, a blessing is described as an act of seeking or giving (esp. divine) favour.

Over the years I have seen many people have amazing results with blessings in their health and lives.

If you have a particular negative issue in your life, e.g. ill health, fallen out with a family member, or if you have a hospital appointment due about which you are really apprehensive, this is an amazing tool which can help you and if you have enough belief can completely eradicate the problem!

Before you start this process do not worry if you find it hard to visualise. You can still do this process; remember it is your intention which is most important.

Sending a blessing

1. Firstly, sit down in a quiet place and feel in your heart a feeling of pure love (sometimes it helps to place your hand on your heart). Then imagine yourself being completely surrounded by pure love. You will feel a wonderful loving warmth surrounding you. You may see it as a pink or gold mist encapsulating and surrounding you.
2. Next, think of the issue – your illness or the friend or relative you have fallen out with – and see it as a picture in a bubble. The picture can appear still or in motion. If the issue is too traumatic to visualise then simply see the bubble filled with a dark muggy colour and just know this represents the issue.
3. Now imagine a beautiful present wrapped perfectly, and that present is filled with pure love (however you want to imagine love, as hearts or kisses or sparkly lights) but just knowing it is filled with pure love from the divine universe and All that is.
4. Next, see that present go above your picture in the bubble. Now pull the ribbon with your mind and see the present open and tip over the picture. See all of the pure love completely cover and fill the whole picture so that the situation has been engulfed in a blessing of pure love and say the words, "I bless this situation with pure love from the divine universe and All that is. Thank you."
5. Now close that picture and know it has been blessed in pure love from the universe. And most importantly say

thank you at least three times to the universe/God/source energy for sending the love.

The important part here is every time you think of the situation, know and completely believe in your heart that it has been blessed in pure love and see it as being perfectly resolved. No longer see it as a negative situation, just imagine a harmonious result. Do not in any way start mulling over the issue; if thoughts of the issue keep popping up in your mind immediately replace them with thoughts of knowing the situation has completely been blessed and resolved.

You only need to do this process once, then, it is imperative you let go of the issue and have complete and absolute faith in knowing it has been blessed by source energy. Sometimes you may find yourself doing the process again, which is fine, but a blessing is a blessing and once done is done. Do not hold on to the issue and keep checking or questioning whether it has worked or not because that means you are lacking complete faith. And that is the key. That is the magic in the whole of this process – keeping the faith. So let it go and then when the situation is resolved you will feel overwhelmed with pure love, knowing that you kept the faith.

Remember, we cannot create other people's lives and decide what is best for them, but as long as our intentions are from the heart then the universe will work with us and have the result that is best for both parties. Have faith in the universe. Sometimes the result is not always what we expect but know that it is for the best for us to evolve as souls. You have done your bit which is surrounding it in love, so the outcome will be what it is meant to be. You will be amazed by how that person changes towards you, or how your illness suddenly improves, or the result from the hospital was far better than you anticipated.

Another thing to remember is that if you use this method on friends, who are for example sick, and they have a sudden speedy recovery or a more positive prognosis after you have sent your blessing, you will then realise in your heart how powerful this process is. Sometimes when you tell people they may shun the idea. Do not be disheartened by this. You know, because you are working with the universe, the universe is working with you. Do not dwell on trying to prove to people it works. If they are open to this then they will ask you and you can help them to work with this concept if it is new to them. If they are closed and negative you will never convince them so do not get involved in lengthy negative debates. Just smile and know they have a slightly longer journey than you, and when they are ready they too will work with the universe.

It doesn't have to be a negative situation. You can use blessings on anything and everything. You could think of your children and see them blessed every day, or your partner, health, home or food. Or just begin every day with a special blessing to your day ahead. How wonderful it feels to know your day has already been blessed before you have even got out of bed!

Also, every night before you go to sleep, bless the day that has just passed. If anything didn't go how you wanted it to or negative things happened in your day, just send a blessing and it will wipe the slate clean. This may sound ludicrous but as with everything in this book, just try it and see the results for yourself. You may have had a disagreement with someone that day and go to bed in a very negative mode, mulling over the argument. Instead just imagine you both agree to disagree and send a blessing. You will be overwhelmed by the result.

This is a powerful process, enjoy it and have complete faith.

In brief:

➣ *Familiarise yourself with this chapter so that you completely understand how it works.*

➣ *A blessing can be used on anything or anyone. It is a very powerful way of sending love from the universe.*

➣ *The most important part of this process is to have absolute faith.*

➣ *Enjoy this wonderful gift.*

CHAPTER 20

Living the dream is… knowing love will always conquer fear

Love and fear are constantly in our thoughts. Love is all the wonderful things in our life, all the things we truly appreciate – our families, health, home etc. It is what inspires us and it makes us feel fantastic. Fear is all the things that we have no power over and therefore we feel threatened by. Fear is very powerful and we thrive on it. You only have to look at top selling books, DVDs and console games to see many top sellers are extremely negative. Horrors, murders, abuse etc. Newspaper headlines will often be negative and if there is a crisis, then we can't buy enough or listen to enough of it. It is not the newspapers' fault – they only go by demand and there is certainly demand for it.

Some people live their whole lives in fear, worrying that

something terrible could happen to them. When you are young you think you are immortal but suddenly after you have children, you live in fear that something terrible could happen to you. We start to think, *What if I have a brain tumour or some incurable disease or a heart attack?* Fear can rule your life if you let it. It is very powerful, and for people who have panic attacks and phobias it does rule their life. We only fear because it is the unknown, we have no control over it and we worry it will take over and we will be at its mercy.

We have all seen programmes where people confront their fears and actually overcome them. It is you who created the fear. It is you who has given it power. Some people have a fear of heights, some of spiders, but most people don't. So therefore it is not the actual thing that is fearful, it is the thought that only you have given it. So if it is a thought that has created the fear then of course a thought can be undone. Change the thought to what you want it to be. Obviously for people who have a lifelong phobia it can take a bit of time, but the point I'm trying to make is, it is 'your thought' that is the problem, not the actual issue. The more energy you put into that thought then the bigger the fear. Work on that thought and realise it is you who is causing the fear to yourself, it is not the object doing it. The thought and the object are two completely different things, it is only you that has connected the two. Usually from an experience you may remember, or could well have forgotten. Send a blessing in chapter 19 and if it is a deep-rooted fear from a trauma that happened to you, then work on chapter 18 on forgiveness and letting go. Some people think tarantulas are scary, some people think they are cute and cuddly – they are neither. They are whatever each individual believes them to be.

A simple process to overcome your fear is to think of your fear. For example, spiders. Research and get as much information as possible to find out how truly amazing they really are. Print and cut out cute cartoons and pictures of spiders. Do not do any negative research whatsoever. If a negative page does come up immediately change pages and keep researching all the wonderful and positive things about them. Your brain is like a computer so the more information you get, the more is being stored until you have tipped the scales onto the positive side. Then of course you start to be amazed by spiders because in your brain the positives outweigh the negatives. It is the same with absolutely anything, which is why we can all retrain our brain and mindset. It is purely the information that is held within us that helps us to decide. Like a mini jury inside our brain. Any situation or belief can be changed, all you have to do is research all the positives in that situation and not acknowledge any of the negatives, it really is that simple. There will always be as many negatives as positives but why would you want to torture yourself? You have nothing to gain but more misery. It is the negatives that created the fear in the first place.

Obviously if there was a trauma that created this fear, like your lovely brother throwing a spider in your face or down your top when you were little, then yes, of course you will have a fear, but it can still be overcome. You just need to do a bit more research to tip the scales. Even if your phobia almost killed you, it didn't, so it can still be overcome. When people face their fears head-on, the brain has to make a quick decision – fight or flight. We have an adrenaline rush which can either be turned to a positive or negative and in most cases we decide to stand our ground (or fight). Your brain has to immediately move to a different concept and suddenly we feel immense power because we have faced our fear and won. The positive feeling has far outweighed the negative, we have overcome our fear. Every time we now think of it, we feel positive instead of negative.

If you suffer from panic attacks then once again it is the amount of energy you give it that gives the attack the power. Remember, a panic attack cannot kill you. Instead of feeding the fear remember nothing can ever be more powerful than love. Only focus on the love within you. Only focus on your soul which is pure love. Your body is an illusion. For the moment during an attack, treat it like an old friend and say, "OK, it's *just* a panic attack." Do not acknowledge the attack, just hand it over to your soul. Send a blessing and only imagine you are a pure soul surrounded in pure love. If that is your one and only thought, a panic attack can no longer exist because it is a physical response. Your soul is not physical, so the attack cannot affect you because your soul is the real you. A panic attack is merely your ego feeding the fear on a physical level which creates the physical response of the attack. Absolutely nothing can ever be more powerful and pure than your soul, most certainly never any ego.

For a lot of us, our biggest fear is dying because it is something we have no control over. None of us know the date that has been set. Some people believe we have three dates set and we can overcome the first two. Or maybe sometimes our soul may feel ready to go home and be free of pain emotionally and physically. Personally, I believe this to be true. I think our soul has a choice of death departures, with the final being in old age. This explains why some people overcome an illness deemed incurable and others don't. None of us will know our dates. The very reason we don't know is what keeps us on our toes. It is to help us live every moment to the full, and if that is how you live, then you will have no fear of dying because you will have lived the life of your dreams with no regrets. Can you imagine if we were all told we would die on the day we reached 100 years old? What a procrastinating lot we would be. Everything could be put off until tomorrow because there would certainly be plenty of them! Appreciate and give thanks that we don't know, instead of fretting and suffering anxiety over it. Have faith that source energy is a far greater intelligence than us and only has our interests as evolving souls at heart.

When people do pass over then know that was their time. It was their special date. Of course it doesn't make it easier for those left behind, but that's the way it works, it is absolute perfection.

So as always, everything is whatever you believe it to be. Which would you rather be – someone who lives in the belief they are surrounded by pure love, or someone who lives in fear? Any fear can always be overcome by injecting love into the situation. The choice is yours.

In brief:

~ *Realise there is nothing to fear, only your thought. It is 'your thought' that makes something fearful, not the actual thing. So change 'your thought'.*

~ *Research all the positives until you tip the scales, then you will convince the jury in your mind.*

~ *In any situation, love will always conquer fear.*

CHAPTER 21

Living the dream is… knowing love is eternal

We have all experienced love at some point in our lives. For most of us it starts from a very young age which is the love from our parents; the love of mother and child is such a special and powerful love. Then we have our family pets: dogs, cats, horses etc. It is an independent love away from our parents. Our pets can show us unconditional and unselfish love. No matter what we have done or said they absolutely adore us and our special canine will always greet us with a wagging tail. Their loyalty is exceptional and we have so much to learn from our pets. They are one of our greatest teachers and instead of us trying to teach them new tricks, take a step back and let them teach you their wonderful gift of kindness. Some of us may find true love in our partners with whom we feel we would like to spend the rest of our lives. Some of us fall out of love, move on and find love with someone else.

But because we are here in physical form, we all know and all agree that one day our mortal body will die. Every single living thing on this planet will eventually die.

It is at this point that many people have different viewpoints. Some people believe that is it, no more, nothing. Most religions believe we pass over to the afterlife dependant on what denomination you are. But because all of these are belief systems of pure faith we find it hard to know what really happens, because there is no scientific proof. Many people have had NDEs (near death experiences). But scientifically we are told it is because a chemical, Dimethyltryptamine or DMT, is released from the pineal gland in the brain when the heart stops that creates the illusion of passing over. But those who have experienced NDEs are absolutely adamant that they had a very real experience which prompted them to completely reassess their lives, or never have any fear of dying after because they have seen with their very eyes that the afterlife does exist.

Many of us have lost someone close, either a relative or an adored pet. There is an insufferable pain that we feel when this happens. It literally feels like your heart is breaking. Gradually as time goes by we learn to live without our loved one and the pain eases. If it is a young person or a shock accident, some people who had faith in God or a religion will shun their belief and disregard it totally, believing that if a child or parent of children can die, then this can be no God of love. They want nothing more to do with it, which then results in even more pain and loneliness because there is now nowhere left to turn.

This is a very controversial subject but the reason I am mentioning this, is that if you are carrying this pain and hate and it is not released it will eat away at you and you will live the rest of your life in trauma, emotionally and physically.

You will never forget your loved one but there is a way to learn to live with their physical death. We feel so much pain because we feel they have gone. We will never physically see them again and if we have no belief in the afterlife then it is quite unbearable to think that we will never ever meet up again.

Our soul is eternal. If you have worked with the methods in this book you have been working with your soul. When someone passes over it is merely a transition and their first and foremost concern is for you, their loved one.

If you sit quietly and surround yourself with a feeling of pure love you will feel their presence. They will send you little messages of comfort. Open yourself up to this, I have heard such heart-warming stories when people open themselves up. As they have gone about their day they have seen such special little things which they know can only be from their loved one. Another way is to write a letter to them and say all the things you felt you never said, but wished you had. Tell them how much you love them and miss them or whatever you feel in your heart. Maybe wrap a ribbon around your letter and keep it in a special place with a photo of them or the two of you together. Plant something in your garden which blooms a beautiful flower. Talk to them and know they can hear you. If you are really struggling and feel strong angry emotions to your loved one because they have left you all alone and you miss them so terribly, or they passed away suddenly without having a chance to say goodbye, then write it down. Say everything you feel, do not feel guilty about being angry with them, this is perfectly natural. Let it all out as described in chapter 18 – Forgiveness and letting go. Then when you have finished, destroy the letter. You will feel quite emotional, but also a huge relief. Do this as many times as you feel the need. You will feel an immense release.

Now I can assure you none of this is spooky stuff, it is just pure love connecting to you so you can move on in your life and let go of the pain and torment. Know it was their time, they had done what they had come to do. Learn and be inspired from their life, that is how they would want to be remembered, not to leave pain and suffering. Of course you miss them but when you see little signs it will help you so much to know they have passed over to a place of pure love. They are now free souls and one day you will meet again when your time comes.

Remember, love and your soul are eternal and will always exist.

In brief:

If you have lost someone close and are suffering, then use this chapter to help you deal with the grief and know that your loved one will always be. They have merely passed over from this physical world into the realm of pure love and when your time comes then you will meet again.

LIVING THE DREAM IS...

~ Love is the most powerful energy that exists and will always exist.

CHAPTER 22

Living the dream is… knowing how to heal yourself

This chapter is in no way written to offend anyone. It is written to give hope and inspiration to people who are suffering.

Anyone can heal themselves.

Yes, believe it or not you possess everything you need to heal yourself. How exciting is that? Whatever the prognosis, you always have a choice – to completely recover.

People all over the world cure themselves daily even when they have been told there is no hope. A so-called 'miraculous recovery' that science has no explanation for.

So how can this be? Well, the answer is simple. All of these people had one thing in common – they had complete faith in their recovery, irrelevant of whether it was conventional, alternative or self-healing, they completely believed in a positive outcome, they only saw the end result and truly believed they would be healed. They did not acknowledge the illness in any way, shape or form, only focused on a healthy body. So the most important part of this process is complete faith and belief in your healing, not only on a conscious level but a knowing from deep within your heart and soul.

If you find this difficult to grasp then do your own research. Read up about people who overcome the 'impossible'. You will find the same answer with each and every one of their stories. Every single one believed in their healing.

This is why some therapies and surgeries work for some people and not for others. It is not the therapy or the procedure that takes place, it is how much belief you have in it that makes it a success or not. This is why the practitioner or surgeon plays a huge role in your recovery. If they do not have faith in your recovery then you are pretty much on to a nonstarter. How can a patient have faith if the practitioner doesn't? You would have to have an extremely powerful mindset to overcome your practitioner's belief. But many people do, and that is when it is called a miraculous recovery. It happened purely because the patient believed in their recovery 100%. (If you need a scientific explanation for this I strongly recommend you read *You Are the Placebo* by Dr Joe Dispenza. He explains scientifically with proof of brain scans how a prolonged thought actually creates signals to the cells which then go on to create new genes, so that the healing can take place and health is completely restored. All of his case studies, including himself, made miraculous recoveries.)

Another example of this is *the placebo effect* where the patient is unknowingly given a sugar pill for a particular condition. The results are the same if not sometimes better than the actual prescribed drug for that condition. The only explanation for a successful result is purely from the belief of the patient's mind.

As soon as you give your illness thought, you give it energy. The more energy you give it, the more it comes into existence. The greatest thing that feeds it is fear. Fear is such a powerful energy; the more you think about it, the greater it becomes. When you have an illness, instead of hating your body or wondering why it has done this to you, thank it. Remember your body is your loyal servant, it serves you unconditionally to the very end. If you hate your body or the part of your body where the illness resides then you are hating yourself. Your body is you. How can you work with yourself and heal with love if you hate yourself? An illness is your body telling you it is suffering a trauma, either physically or emotionally. Work with your body and nurture it. Remember chapter 13 – Your body is your temple. Send pure love to the part of your body that is suffering and imagine your body starting to heal itself, do not acknowledge the illness, only acknowledge a healing process taking place. Remember, love is all you need; you come from love, the universe, get on the same frequency and work with it. Send a blessing in chapter 19 and work on chapter 18 – Forgiveness and letting go.

An illness can only stay in your body through thought. The thought has to be changed from believing the illness is part of you and holding it there through fear of what it can do to you, to being free of the illness. And remember, feelings play a major role so if you feel fear or negative energy towards it then that is what will keep it there. You have to feel excited about being free of the ailment so that the excitement outweighs the fear. Do not acknowledge negative thoughts. Every time you think of your body, only focus on the end result that you want to see. Do not think of the negative result. Only focus on your perfect loyal body which is protecting you. You never look at healing a cut as being miraculous but think about it, it is a pure miracle how it clots the blood and it seals itself back together. Scientific version:

- Vasoconstriction – blood vessels leading to the wound tighten to reduce the flow of blood to the injured area.
- Platelets (triggered by enzymes leaked from the torn blood vessel) rush to the scene. These sticky blood cells clump to each other and then adhere to the sides of the torn blood vessel, making a plug.
- Clotting proteins in the blood join forces to form a fibrin net that holds the platelet blood in place over the tear, and in just a few seconds or minutes, bleeding stops. This is called coagulation. The fibrin plug becomes a scab that will eventually fall off or be reabsorbed into the body once healing is complete.

Once bleeding is controlled the next step is stopping infection. And so the next complex process takes place until our amazing body has performed another miracle, which we have simply taken completely for granted.

Just imagine for a moment if the whole process of healing from open bleeding wound to skin completely back to normal took 20 seconds. You would stand there with a dropped jaw and think some kind of magic had taken place. So why are we not amazed just because it takes a couple of days rather than a few seconds? The process is still the same. So of course your body can heal anything, and it does. It has everything it needs to heal any ailment you can ever have. If you need proof of this then research how truly miraculous the human body is. All it needs is the go-ahead from you, which is love and belief. Have faith in the perfection of your body and give thanks for it, it is your one and only.

As I mentioned at the beginning of the chapter, none of this is written to offend. If you have an illness or have been involved in an accident then of course you didn't consciously intend this to happen. But you can overcome anything or learn to live a better life with belief and a positive mindset. Just try it. Give yourself at least a month and you will begin to see changes, then you will have the proof.

As we get older we become sceptical. We have to let go of this mindset. Children respond so well to suggestion because they are not sceptical. When one of my sons was young we noticed a great big painful verruca on the bottom of his foot. I decided to work on suggestion. When my son went up to bed I said to him we would not look at the bottom of his foot for seven days and the next time we looked at it, the verruca would be gone. So seven days later we went up to bed and checked the foot; we saw a great big hole already starting to close up where the verruca had been. My son had just completely believed what I had said. There was no hope or wishful thinking. I had simply told him, when we look in seven days it will be gone, and he completely believed that, so therefore it was gone.

Take responsibility for your health. Almost every ailment can be helped immensely by proper diet and exercise. If you are receiving treatment, work with it but also do your own research, look for alternative methods and diets recommended for your condition. This will give you so much more confidence in the healing because you are doing everything you can to help the healing take place.

As described in chapter 2 – Taking a step back, your body's healing process excels when you are balanced and happy. As you are healing, only watch funny films and listen to things that make you laugh. Surround yourself in a positive and happy environment; do not acknowledge any negativity in your life, then your body can happily focus on the healing process.

Stress is a drain on your body and will slow down the healing. Do not give a single second thought to a negative outcome. If negative thoughts do come into your mind then just gently push them away, and keep refocusing on the positive outcome and get *excited* about the end result.

Your body is replacing around 50 billion cells a day. So if you can imagine all of your cells are created and filled daily with healing love, the effects are mind-blowing. Imagine this amazing healing taking place. Imagine every breath you take is a healing, loving, positive breath and every breath out is all the negativity and stale illness coming out and being released into the universe to be transformed into pure loving energy. Doesn't this feel absolutely fantastic? Get really *excited* about your healing. Your body is healing every second and your loving thoughts have a profound effect.

Whenever I get stressed or feel myself getting worked up or anxious I always remind myself that whoever or whatever is causing your stress is never worth your health. If you can feel yourself getting worked up then you are already releasing negative energy and chemicals in your body. Is it worth it? Is it really worth your health?

Another important thing to remember is an illness is usually (not always) an emotional imbalance or trauma that has, over a period of time, manifested as a physical issue. So when you use this process for the healing, it is important that any emotional traumas or skeletons in your cupboard are released. Work on chapter 18 – Forgiveness and letting go. This is why some people overcome illnesses but then the illness may come back. It is because they have not released the emotional trauma that caused the illness in the first place. If you're thinking, *Well how am I supposed to know what has caused this?* think carefully. Firstly, if you are suffering a severe and aggressive illness then you usually have suffered a pretty severe emotional trauma and it won't take a lot of effort to work out what it was (remember, this could even be something that happened in your childhood which you have managed to live with, but maybe now you have children it has come to the forefront of your mind). Less severe ailments will be less severe traumas but obviously enough to cause an ailment. It could even be the trauma your partner brings home to you every day like verbal abuse, insults etc. It could be you are unhappy at work. You will know because when you think of the issue it is enough for you to feel a physical response (like a negative flutter in your tummy or your heart races). Usually an illness will appear about 6-12 months after the trauma. When you feel you have got through the trauma and are getting back to so-called normality then the illness will quite often rear its ugly head.

I'm not saying every negative thing in your life will cause an illness. Most things that wind us up are in the moment, then we move on and forget about it in a day, a week, or a month or two (if it goes on longer than this then you really need to work on releasing it). It is an issue that will have manifested over a prolonged period that has caused us anxiety or maybe a severe shock, which we may react to instantly, or over a period of time. You now have the tools in this book so use them as often as you need. Below are the steps for the healing process.

Healing Process

Step 1 – Thank your body for telling you there is an imbalance.
Step 2 – Think of that part of your body and focus on it

being surrounded by pure love. If you are receiving treatment then have total faith in the treatment. Send blessings, chapter 19, and every time you think of it know it has been blessed in the pure love from the universe. Have complete faith and belief in this knowledge.

Step 3 – Imagine for just one second actually not having the illness, your body only being healthy. Keep practising this as often as you can then progress to two seconds and keep progressing. Each time you do this, feel really excited about being free of your illness. You are firstly tricking your conscious mind into thinking you do not have the illness for one second, and the more you progress with time the more it becomes reality and your existence.

Step 4 – Only focus on the end result you want to see; picture it and keep imagining you're already there. Really feel what it feels like to have the outcome you want and get so excited about it. When you genuinely feel these feelings, it means you are almost there – it is becoming your reality. You must have complete faith in the outcome, not hoping it may happen, but complete belief and that inner *knowing* that it will. Remember, you are the creator of your world, whatever you believe will be your reality.

Step 5 – You have arrived! The timescale of healing was the amount of energy and belief you gave to this process. Give thanks to the universe and your body, you are truly blessed.

Some of you may get an instant result. For some of you, time is involved. If time is involved then do not fret. Just keep focusing on the end result and have total belief. Be at peace with yourself and have total faith in your perfect healing body and the blessings of the universe. Sometimes the ailment may seem to be getting worse or not going away, this is just your body readjusting, or the 'healing crisis' where the ailment has to get worse before it gets better because the healing has been given a huge surge forward. Remember not to acknowledge this, just focus on the end result you wish to see. Give as much positive energy as you can and just go with however long it takes. Most importantly, do not fight the illness. Many people say, "I'm going to fight this thing." But then you are fighting yourself. It is your body which has created the illness to tell you there is an imbalance. You have to work with your body and the healing process with pure love and positivity. Not with anger and hate, or the negativity will keep being reflected back into your life. Use the fighting energy like an athlete and turn it to a positive, but instead of running a marathon, use it as a huge surge of healing.

You can also use this process on other people, which will help them immensely. But you cannot determine their outcome. That is their journey. Help them by keeping them positive and showing them the way. Another thing to remember is that some people don't actually want to be healed. This may sound crazy but some people consciously and some unconsciously actually nurture their illness. Without it they wouldn't get the attention or the benefits that come with the illness. Some people actually enjoy the appointments with the doctors, consultants etc. Some people who may have felt hard done by or that they've had a difficult life, can actually thrive on the demands they can now make on friends, relatives and health professionals. I have seen many people who suffer this fate. They come to be healed but when they realise how very different their life would be, sheer panic can come over them when they realise they could suddenly be independent and go out to work and drive themselves around. Of course this group is in the minority but the majority of those people don't even realise they are in this group. The point I am trying to make is, if the healing process is to take place then you have to be honest with yourself – do you really want to be healed? A quick way to find the answer is to imagine being totally free of your ailment. How does this feel? If you truly and genuinely feel so happy to be free of it and can actually imagine for a second not having the illness, then you want to be healed. If you start to feel anxiety at the very thought, then you need to really think long and hard about the outcome.

Another group is those people who want to be healed but don't believe anything or anyone can heal them. They have doomed themselves to the fate of the illness. You have to completely open your mind and let go of limited beliefs for your sake.

The healing cannot take place until the person wants to be

healed and actually *believes* they can be healed with all of their heart.

If you are open to this then read on and learn hands-on healing.

There are so many forms of conventional and alternative healing. A simple and effective form is hands-on healing. Anyone can use this. It is merely channelling pure love from the universe. It cannot harm you because your intention is merely channelling pure love. The reason healing takes place during or after the treatment is because, as with everything, we respond positively to pure love and when this is channelled through we feel at peace and our body starts to rebalance itself, and healing naturally takes place.

Hands-on healing

1. Wash your hands.
2. Cleanse the room either with an incense stick or with your intention (believe and feel it being cleansed of any negativity). You may also light a candle and put some gentle music on. Then imagine the room or area filled with love.
3. Simply sit quietly and be in your own space and feel yourself surrounded by pure love.
4. It is important to ground yourself, so imagine for a moment your feet are like the roots of a tree and go deep down into the earth's core.
5. You may lie or sit, whichever is most comfortable to you. Now say to yourself, "I connect in love and light to the

pure healing energy of the divine universe and All that is."
6. Now very gently place your hands on your head and hold them there. You may get sensations in your hands and this may vary. You will usually feel heat, sometimes cold, sometimes a pulse from one hand to the other. This is all fine, just relax and enjoy the experience. Hold them there for five to ten minutes or for as long as you feel the need, then move to your breast bone. Hold them there for five to ten minutes or as long as you feel the need, then move them to your abdomen. Hold them there for five to ten minutes or as long as you feel the need. If you feel drawn to any particular areas then just move your hands to that area and simply follow your instinct and let the healing flow.
7. Always keep your hands connected to the body. If for some reason you are drawn away like answering the telephone etc. (although try to switch distractions off), when you go back, say, "I reconnect in love and light." Or if you feel your mind has wandered away from the healing then bring yourself back into the moment and say, "I reconnect in love and light and to the pure healing energy of the divine universe and All that is."
8. When you have finished, place your hands back on your head and say, "Thank you for this healing, I disconnect in love and light." Always give thanks to divine source energy.
9. It is important to wash your hands before and after healing as a disconnection and cleansing technique.

This is a very relaxing and enjoyable experience for everyone, whether you are healing yourself or someone else (animals also love it). Just stay in the moment and relax and enjoy it.

In brief:

◦ *You possess everything you need to heal yourself but the number one ingredient you must have is belief.*

◦ *Do not fight the illness. It is your body that has created the illness to tell you there is an imbalance. If you fight it you are fighting yourself. Thank your body and work with pure love in the healing process.*

◦ *It is important to work on the emotional trauma that has created the illness and to release it so your body can recover quickly and the illness will not return.*

◦ *Do you or they really want to be healed?*

◦ *Practise the healing technique. Even if you don't need healing it is an extremely relaxing experience.*

CHAPTER 23

Living the dream is… being true to yourself

The only reason we suffer in this life, either emotionally or physically, is because we are not living our lives to the full, we are not being true to ourselves. For some people their lives have already been decided by their parents or guardians. If there is a family business then it is usually presumed that their offspring will take over the empire. If the parents either have, or have had a particular career sometimes they decide that is also best for their children, or maybe they think they should be a teacher, doctor, policeman etc., and so it goes on.

Some people are with partners because other people think they should be together. Some people choose not to have children, buy a house or a car or live in an area purely because someone else thinks it would be better for them.

Therefore, many of us are living lives to keep other people happy. If you are not happy from within, it is because you are not living the life you want to live. There are no excuses. You make the choice. If you are not happy, then it is you who has put yourself there. You cannot blame other people for your life. If you live a miserable existence because you did what other people told you to do, take responsibility for your life. Only you know what is best for you. If you live from your heart then you will follow your dreams. Your soul is your guide, listen to it. It knows what you love. And of course, if you do what you love then you will be extremely successful at it. Nobody is successful at something if they don't enjoy it. You have to do what you love otherwise you will live an unhappy life because you will not be fulfilling your life's ambition and journey. If you are at a place right now, with huge responsibilities and a family to feed, yet you long for a career change, there is always a way. The universe will work with you if you follow your heart. The doors will open. Have faith and believe.

We spend our lives doing what we think is best and worrying what the neighbours or our parents or family will say. You end up like a dog chasing his tail because you are trying to keep everyone happy but yourself. Just live from your heart and follow your dreams and do what you truly want to do. You owe it to yourself. The knock-on effect is when you're happy, then all of your family will be happy because you will no longer be a stressed-out parent or partner. Then you can help your friends and family to find their happiness too.

In brief:

➣ *Live your life, not someone else's.*
➣ *Your soul is your guide. It knows what you love. Listen to it.*
➣ *Follow your dreams and with them will come contentment and joy.*

CHAPTER 24

Living the dream is... knowing you are an evolving soul

In almost every chapter in this book I have referred to our soul. That is basically all that we are. Our physical form is an illusion. It has been given to us in this life so that we can experience physical sensations, that is why we are capable of healing our bodies because it doesn't really exist, it is only an energy form under a microscope as described in chapter 9 – Working with the law of attraction. An illness is a negative thought pattern held in certain areas of the body which, if not resolved, becomes physical manifestations, so by changing the thought pattern or letting go of the issue, the illness disappears.

In every situation in our life we have a choice and it is up to us to decide. Ideally the choice we take in every situation should be from our heart but very often we take the logical route which our ego tells us should be the right answer, after which we will usually gain some reward to boost our ego. But it is very simple, just live from your heart and that is always the right answer. Our soul is evolving, that is why we are here. We have a lot to learn. There are some enlightened beings who walk amongst us. They are very humble beings who only live from their hearts. Be inspired by them, learn from them. You have the greatest guide within you, it has every answer you need, but you have to listen, you have to take a step back and know you have this pure love within you that is here to guide you and wants to shine through you, but only you can give it that power. When you do, you will shine like the purest diamond and be an absolute joy to be around.

Know now that you are a soul in a physical body, not a physical body with a soul. Know that you will be, forever. Yes, your physical body will eventually die, but your soul will go on through many lifetimes, evolving until source energy feels you have evolved in the physical world and will then become a guide for other souls on their journey. Believe you are truly special because you are. You chose, with source energy, to live this life, so live it to the full so you can evolve. You may go on a quest in search of source energy. Is there a god, source, that you can pray or talk to? That is fine, but only go with what feels right and comfortable with you. Know that wherever you go or whatever route you take should only resonate pure love. Do not feel you have to go to some sweat lodge or start praying to full moons. If you are genuinely living from your heart and you are seeing the magic in your life then you are just as evolved spiritually as a guru with a title to their name. You must go with what feels instinctively right with you. It should only resonate pure love. If it feels uncomfortable or negative then it is not right for you. Just do what you feel completely at peace with.

You now know there is an unstoppable force that wants you to live from your heart and will open every door for you if you do, but you may want to know more. You now know there is an intelligence that is far greater than we can even begin to imagine. When we work with it, it will carry us in the palm of its hand. When we work against it, we will live an unhappy existence. Some people call this Karma.

There is only so much we will ever know, no matter how deep our quest. Nobody actually knows what happens after an NDE – that is the furthest we have gone. We find it very hard in this world to believe if we do not have scientific proof, but of course spirituality can never be proved. It is something so pure it has nothing to do with science or logic. It is simply a feeling. A feeling that is held deep within our soul and when we work with it, it is like living in another world. Do not worry about people who mock this belief. Just know you are blessed and be as loving as you can and your journey will be more than any words can describe. It will be the purest feeling you can ever imagine. And we know the more we live from our hearts, the more magic we see.

You may not need to search. Just meditating and connecting to source energy, being at one with nature or a simple prayer gives you all the confirmation you need to know you are blessed and are surrounded by the purest love.

Never underestimate the power of prayer. Anyone who has achieved fantastic things and their ambitions in this life will nearly always admit to working with God or source energy. You will see them giving thanks or praying before or after a big event. Many famous footballers, actors, singers or top athletes will all admit to having help from above. They know the power of prayer. They know true inspiration comes from pure love which is of course, source energy.

In brief:

Know you are an evolving soul.

Remember you are a soul in a physical body, not a physical body with a soul.

If you feel you need to go on a spiritual quest, only go with what feels comfortable to you. If it feels negative then this is not source energy. You should only feel pure love in you quest.

CHAPTER 25

Living the dream is... detachment

Many of us have possessions in life. A big house, an expensive car, jewellery etc.

The problem with possessions is, they can give the owner a sense of power. The more they own the more powerful they think they become, where in fact it is quite the opposite. The possession becomes the owner of you, it has a hold on you. Success is quite often measured in material possessions. If someone has a big house we tend to think, *Oh, they must be very successful*.

Success should always be measured by a peaceful soul. If someone has complete inner peace then that is success. They have succeeded in all the challenges in life. They do not need possessions to make them happy because they have found themselves. They feel peace in every situation because they have fed their soul. They have complete inner peace and live only from their heart.

There is nothing wrong with ambition, but only if it genuinely makes you happy and you're not doing it to prove a point, for example to a family member who said you would never amount to anything or a sibling who gloated in their higher achievements. Ambition should always be from inspiration or it won't last and you will never find satisfaction in your success. There is nothing wrong with expensive material possessions, but only if they genuinely make you happy.

If there was no one else in the world, would you really be bothered about having a big house or fancy clothes?

We hold on to things to give us an identity and we expect them to make us feel good. All of this attaches us to our so-called belongings. It means we give power to objects and are very needy. We have lost control of our real power which is finding our bliss and making ourselves happy. We expect objects to make us happy.

Some of us may expect people, our partners or children, to make us happy or tend to our needs. It is only you who is responsible for your life, nobody else. Do not lay blame or make demands from other people. You must find your joy. You must find your bliss.

Material things can be fun but just be aware to work on yourself first and be happy from within. Love yourself and be at peace with yourself, then have material things as a bit of fun. Do not give them the power to own you. You are responsible for your own joy.

Of course it is only you that knows what you truly want

and love. So detach yourself, take a step back and love and give thanks for your blessed life.

In brief:

↣ *Be aware of possessions. Who owns who?*

↣ *Imagine every night before you go to sleep not owning one single possession. Imagine just you and the universe as one. That is the most powerful feeling of inner strength and peace that any millions of possessions could never give you.*

↣ *Do not expect possessions or people to create your happiness. Only you are responsible for your feelings. You will never find long-term happiness and peace from material objects. Find your bliss and feed your soul first, then material objects are the icing on the cake.*

CHAPTER 26

Living the dream is… knowing your life is a mirror image of your thoughts

When you look at your life what do you see? Do you see happiness, health and a wonderful life? Or do you see sadness, illness and a depressing life? When you look at the world around you what do you see? Do you see a kind, loving and generous world? Or do you see pain, torture, cruelty, deceit and debt?

Your world is whatever you perceive it to be. It is your choice. You can look around you and feel totally blessed or you can look around you and see a horrific and scary world. Why would you choose the latter? Yes, natural or manmade disasters can happen but it is how we deal with them that make us who we are and the kind of world we live in. If we all start to listen to our soul and live from our hearts then we can all overcome anything. After reading the chapters in this book you have now come to realise you create your world. Whatever your thoughts and energy are focused upon is the results you will see.

Many of you may not have been aware of this concept before and have unconsciously created a life that you may not have chosen. But you now know you are totally responsible for your life and your world through every thought and feeling you experience. How wonderful and exciting to now know that by working with source energy you can create a life and world that you could only have dreamed of. You have the power to create anything you want through your thoughts and actions. The one and only tool you must use is to live from your heart and listen to your wisest guru… your soul. It has always been within you and always will be. We only have one challenge in this life… to let go of our ego.

Become aware of your thoughts and actions because they are creating your reality. The mistake we tend to make is to respond to our circumstances. If it's positive we will be happy. If its negative it makes us sad. We do not seem to realise we create the circumstance in the first place through our energy. If our thoughts and feelings are positive we can only create a positive life. If our thoughts and feelings are negative we can only create a negative life. Cause and effect. It is that simple. Start off by being conscious of your thoughts for 20 seconds; think of positive things and genuinely smile. Then try it for a minute. Then ten minutes, and keep working on yourself until you have made it your habit, until it is ingrained as part of your personality. You will not believe how this will completely transform your whole life and health. If you need proof of this then try it now and be your own guinea pig. It will not take long to convince yourself.

If you become aware of your thoughts and they tend to be quite negative then work on chapters 18 and 19. In the moment, if you catch yourself with negative thoughts stop immediately and say to yourself, "Send love and only love," meaning to send love to that thought so you can let it go, and only love to only think loving thoughts. This is, as always, to free you. To realise the great big mirror of the universe is right there in front of you reflecting every thought in your life. You must become so aware of this.

Another thing to remember is, as described in chapter 1, commitment is vital. As soon as you lapse and get back into your old mindset of negative thinking then of course you will be back to the same life. If you want your life to change you have to commit and change your mindset. Become a people watcher and take note of people's personalities and how their lives pan out. Listen to people in conversation. You will have the positive, health-conscious, aware people who get by pretty well in life. They will always show gratitude for their lives and will appear to be 'lucky' to the negative gang. Then you have the dear old pessimist who will constantly complain about the weather, their health, their neighbour, their family and so on. And of course they will have every health issue going because their poor bodies just are not given the chance to heal through positive mindset. The glass is either half

LIVING THE DREAM IS...

empty or half full. Which one are you?

In brief:

➢ Take a look at your life and world. What do you see?

➢ If you live from your heart and listen to your soul you can overcome anything.

➢ Train your brain to think positive. Start off for 20 seconds then keep building up until it becomes habit. This will transform your life and health.

CHAPTER 27

Living the dream is... knowing life is very simple (a shortcut)

If you see every situation through the eyes of love
If you give thanks daily and show gratitude for your life
If you give generously and genuinely
If you remember you are an evolving soul
If you always live from your heart
If you can live in the very moment and find complete and inner peace
And if above all you have total and complete faith in the divine universe
Then that is the shortcut that will take you to *living the dream.*

It is right here, exactly where you are. It is exactly the same place but in a totally different realm, not because you have moved but because you look at things differently. Because you live from your heart and listen to your soul.

It is a place that is waiting for all of us. And that's all we have to do and the universe will work with us and give us the life of our dreams.

It's that simple. You have joy when you think joy. This is the reason most children are happy, because they look at things differently to us. They look at the world in wonder and have no scepticism or cynicism, they just believe. But as we get older all the negativity slips in; any dreams we had, the doubters saw them off. Look at and research inspirational and successful people and role models. They cast aside all the negativity and ignored all the doubters. They had the big three: love, gratitude, and above all faith in themselves and their dreams.

There are books written about people who are on their deathbed and they tell of their regrets. Don't be one of them. Don't have any regrets when your time comes. Know that you have been true to yourself and lived from your heart, and have done the very best that you can. This life is an absolute blessing. Live your life like it's magic because once you live from your heart, it will be. Yes, you will have challenges, remember to thank them and bless them. Use all the tools in this book and research all the positive things to help you fulfill this life. Do not live a life in fear. Remember, fear is very powerful and if you let it, it will govern your life. Know that nothing is more powerful than love because that is divine source energy. Every single thing you do is your choice. You decide what life you want to lead, do not believe you are a victim of fate. Now picture the life you dream of, and make that dream your reality. You have all of the power you need within you so what are you waiting for? Living the dream is…?

EPILOGUE

This book has been written for anyone and everyone to pick up and read in about an hour or so. The concepts in this book are intended to help you no matter what is going on in your life right now. If they work for you then use them and create yourself an amazing life. If they do not appeal to you then let them go and work with things that do appeal to you at this moment in time.

Ideally read this book through first, then work on each chapter or the ones that appeal to you daily until they become habit.

Thank you for reading this book. May you live the life of your dreams and only see joy and love in each and every moment you are given.

Made in the USA
Columbia, SC
25 July 2018